SOCCER MANIA

ALL-TIME BEST SOCCER TEAMS

Emma Carlson-Berne

Lerner Publications ◆ Minneapolis

To Greg, my favorite soccer player

Statistics in this book are accurate through August 20, 2024.

Copyright © 2026 by Lerner Publishing Group, Inc.

All rights reserved. International copyright secured. No part of this book may be reproduced, stored in a retrieval system, or transmitted in any form or by any means—electronic, mechanical, photocopying, recording, or otherwise—without the prior written permission of Lerner Publishing Group, Inc., except for the inclusion of brief quotations in an acknowledged review.

Lerner Publications Company
An imprint of Lerner Publishing Group, Inc.
241 First Avenue North
Minneapolis, MN 55401 USA

For reading levels and more information, look up this title at www.lernerbooks.com.

Main body text set in Mikado. Typeface provided by HVD fonts.

Editor: Nicole Berglund **Designer:** Viet Chu **Photo Editor:** Nicole Berglund

Library of Congress Cataloging-in-Publication Data

Names: Berne, Emma Carlson, 1979- author.
Title: All-time best soccer teams / Emma Carlson-Berne.
Description: Minneapolis : Lerner Publications , 2025. | Series: Soccer mania (Lerner sports rookie) | Includes bibliographical references and index. | Audience: Ages 5-8 | Audience: Grades K-1 | Summary: "There's no "I" in team! Readers discover popular soccer tournaments and the great pro soccer teams that compete in them"– Provided by publisher.
Identifiers: LCCN 2024038620 (print) | LCCN 2024038621 (ebook) | ISBN 9798765668382 (library binding) | ISBN 9798765683712 (paperback) | ISBN 9798765681138 (epub)
Subjects: LCSH: Soccer—History—Juvenile literature. | Soccer teams—Juvenile literature.
Classification: LCC GV942.5 .B476 2025 (print) | LCC GV942.5 (ebook) | DDC 796.33409—dc23/eng/20241009

LC record available at https://lccn.loc.gov/2024038620
LC ebook record available at https://lccn.loc.gov/2024038621

Manufactured in the United States of America
2-1013184-53806-8/28/2025

Table of Contents

Shoot and Score!   4

Glossary   24
Learn More   24
Index   24

Shoot and Score!

The US Women's National Team was tied with China in the 1999 World Cup. Brandi Chastain booted the ball. The US won!

Long ago, people played soccer with pig bladders stuffed with straw for a ball. Villages played against each other!

Modern soccer began in the 1800s in Britain. The game spread across Europe. Immigrants brought the game to the US.

INSIDE SOCCER

The British first called the game association football.

Pro soccer players play on teams or clubs to win tournaments. Pro players can also play on national teams in the World Cup and the Olympic Games.

FC Barcelona is a team in Spain. They have won more Spanish tournaments than any other team. Lionel Messi played for FC Barcelona from 2004 to 2021.

INSIDE SOCCER

Messi made 672 goals for FC Barcelona, more than any other pro Spanish player.

In 1970, the Brazil men's national team won the World Cup! Their star player, Pelé, wowed the crowd with fancy kicks and passes.

In 1985, the US Women's National Team formed. Since 1991, they have won four World Cups. They have also won five Olympic gold medals.

The US Women's National Team works hard and never gives up. This helps them be one of the best teams in the world.

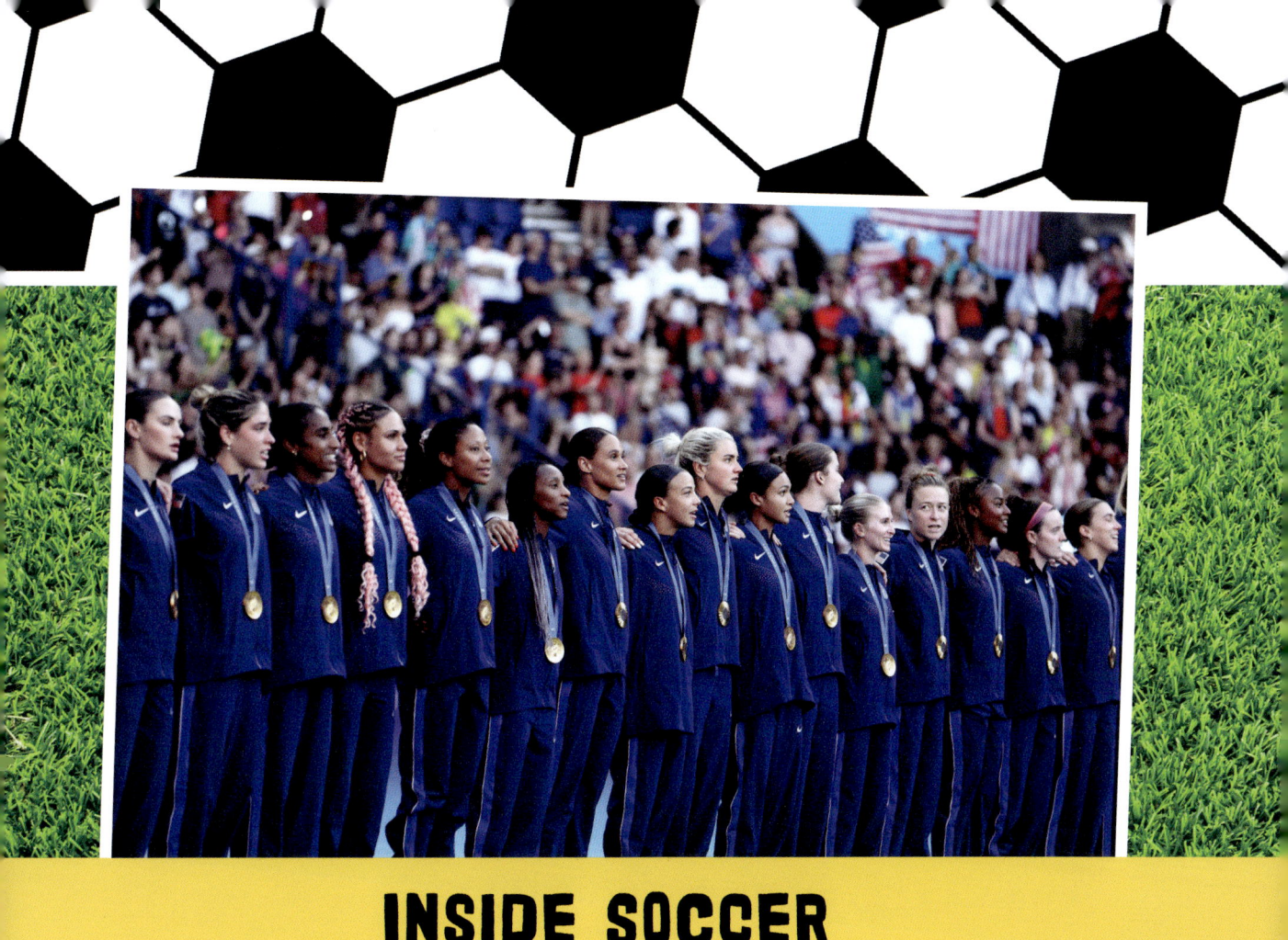

INSIDE SOCCER

The US law Title IX says that female athletes must have the same chances as male athletes.

The Spanish women's national team won the World Cup in 2023. More Spanish people became interested in soccer because of them.

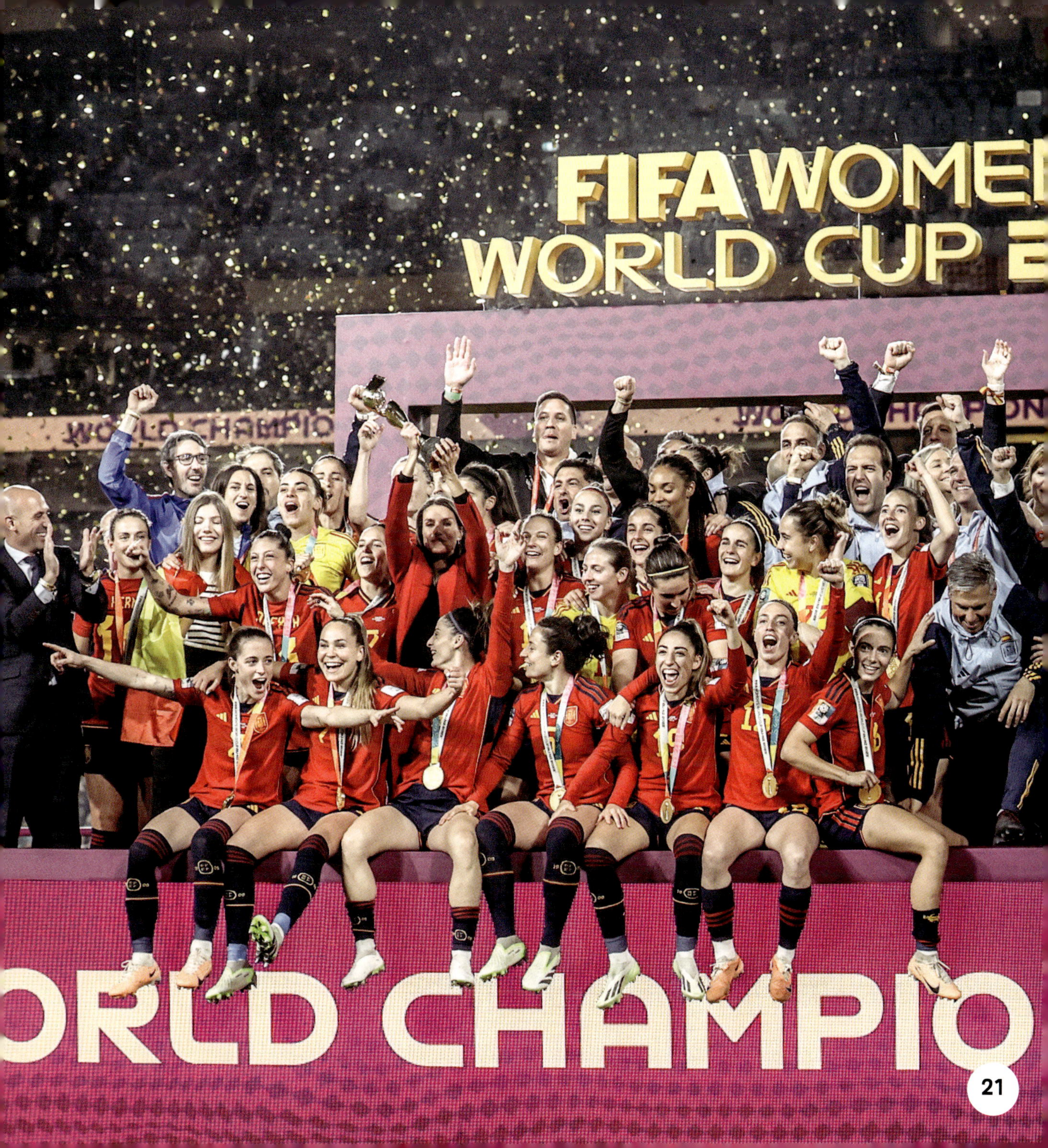
FIFA WOME
WORLD CUP 2
ORLD CHAMPIO

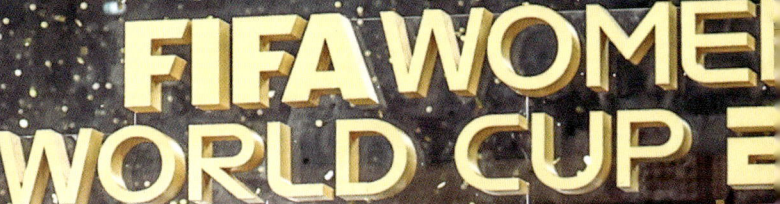

Soccer teams play all over the world. Goalies zip to catch balls. Strikers boot the ball into the net. Let's watch!

Glossary

bladder: a pouch in animals that holds urine

immigrant: a person who moves to another country

national: relating to a whole country or nation

Learn More

Krenn, Cara. *World's Top Soccer Leagues*. Minneapolis: Lerner Publications, 2026.

Laughlin, Kara L. *Soccer*. Parker, CO: Child's World, 2023.

McDougall, Chrös. *Soccer*. Minneapolis: Early Encyclopedias, 2024.

Index

national, 4, 10, 14, 16, 18, 20

Olympic Games, 10, 16

team, 4, 10, 12, 14, 16, 18, 20, 22

tournament, 10, 12

World Cup, 4, 10, 14, 16, 20

Photo Acknowledgments

Image credits: John Todd/ISI Photos/Getty Images, p. 5; Lordprice Collection/Alamy, p. 7; duncan1890/Getty Images, p. 9; AP Photo/Daniela Porcelli/SPP/Sipa USA, p. 11; AP Photo/Manu Fernandez, p. 13; Rolls Press/Popperfoto/Getty Images, p. 15; Al Tielemans/Getty Images, p. 17; Justin Setterfield/Getty Images, p. 19; AP Photo/Patrick Hoelscher/News Images/Sipa USA, p. 21; AP Photo/Press Association, p. 23. Design elements: vid64/Getty Images; boytaro Thongbun/500px/Getty Images. Cover: AP Photo/Joan Valls/Urbanandsport/NurPhoto.